Into the darkness

An insight into the exceptional darkness that lies
hidden within an average man

Michael Griffiths

My lost son and I

The day I lost you, I also lost myself.
You and I stood on the edge of the abyss, and
together we looked over.
With your hand in mine, we fell in and never
stopped falling.
Further and further into the infinite darkness we go.
On the day you died, I died too, I'll never be able to
let you go.
That moment consumes my every thought, it taints
my every feeling.
We are forever falling into the darkness of the
universe.
Destined to be swallowed up and never return.
Your hand in mine for eternity, my son and I
indefinitely lost together.

Daddy still loves you

Will we be able to see each other again?
The Pain in my heart still burns the same
it's been so long
I barely remember your face
Whenever I think of you
My broken heart starts to race
My mind is an inferno
My heart colder than space
The darkness consumes me
Despite my smiling face
Am I destined to relive
That fateful day
When the universe looked down
And swiped you away
My son I love
This I think you know
That day still kills me
The day you had to go
To my forever angel
The guardian of my soul
I'm sorry I never got to you
Before you were cold
Daddy still loves you
And will never let you go

Questions to me

Am I just a number?
What am I worth,
Is my value equal to my impact,
Or am I suffering diminishing returns?

Am I just a name?
How am I defined?
Am I a man of means,
Or the poorest you'll see?

Am I just a resource?
What am I to you?
Do I hold any meaning to you,
Or am I just useful?

Am I just a moment?
How will you remember me?
Will I be thought of fondly,
Or will I just fade into the void of the forgotten past?

Am I really alive?
How do I measure my existence?
Am I truly living,
Or am I merely surviving?

Confidently anxious

Life in this day and age,
Just as it has always been,
Is filled with anxiety, stress, and pain.
Are we enough?
Should we change?
Or is it ok for us to stay the same?
Nobody knows and nobody cares.
Only you can decide,
It's your life and your mind.
Stand on your own two,
Just like they always told you.
With no support can we really thrive?
With no lift from others can we truly fly?
Indecisive in our assertions,
Second guessing our actions.
Our entire existence based on others reactions.
We are an ever growing mess,
Tell me, how are we to make any progress?

My monster, my beast.

They say I have fire in my soul,
They say I have passion in my heart,
But that's only part of me,
Just half of the whole.

Within me lies a monster,
A beast of infinite darkness.
The lighter side of me,
That's my internal fraudster.

There are parts of me that I do not show.
For fear of your reaction,
If you saw the real me,
Surely you would not want to know?

Of myself I am unsure,
If I am truly worthy.
When I look in the mirror I see the monster,
Of this I am sure.

Bumbling, stumbling fool

When I speak I stutter,
As if there is no worth,
To the words that I utter.
My thoughts sound out in a jumble,
A mess that cannot be deciphered or untangled.
My thoughts are clear but my sounds are a
mumble.
If only I could convey my message,
Give to you my thoughtful deliverance.
Instead, I make myself look like I am swimming in
ignorance.
When I write my words are clear,
But you'll never see it because of my fear.
My fear of failure,
My fear of disappointment,
From you, in me.
If only I could share my mind,
So you could see things through my eyes,
So you could feel these feelings of mine.
Because my mouth does not connect to my mind.
My mind is sharp but my voice is weak,
I feel nothing but shame,
When I speak my bumbling speech.

Glass heart

Is it enough that I am me?
Am I really all I can be,
Is there more,
Or am I less.
Do I really have limits,
Or just boundaries to test?
I strive to be better,
But achieve stagnation.
Is this mediocrity really cause for celebration?
I judge myself and I do not pass,
The strength of my heart is brittle like glass.
My soul weeps with pain,
Will it last?
Or is it just another flash in the pan,
A prang in my heart.

Good and evil

Good and evil exists within us all,
Nobody is one of the other.
A line we all share,
A balancing act of biblical proportions.
There is no god,
There is no devil,
There is only us.
Our failings,
Our successes,
Our imperfections.
Only us and our actions.

To be forgotten

We start with nothing,
And we end up with the same.
It's the events in the middle,
That defines the nature of our game.
For some it's intense, fiery and short.
For others it's a careful and considerate walk.
We strive for difference,
Yet we achieve deadly equality.
We try to make our mark,
Just to be remembered.
But in the end we fade,
Like we knew we would from the start.
With nothing left behind,
Not a scrap to be measured.
Is it worth all the effort,
Just to then disappear.
All the pain we experience,
Year upon year.
Should I stop now,o
And just give up here?
Or should I push on,
Despite my desperation and fear?

Undiscovered journey

Life is flowing,
Rapid and uncertain,
Like a river carving it's path through the land.
It twists and it turns,
It relents for no man.
Rapids and waterfalls,
Are all part of the journey.
There's no way to prepare,
So we all set out early.
No matter the course we take,
Or the length of the ride,
Our destination is the same,
We all get there in time.
Some of us fight it,
And that's ok.
While others lay back,
And let it sweep them away.
Do what you want,
Not just what you think you can.
We only ride once,
So be the best person you can.

Shared suffering while you walk alone

When you suffer,
I suffer too.
No matter the situation,
I am right there with you.
When I see the pain in your eyes,
A little more of me dies.

I have failed you,
This I know.
I should have protected you,
But I didn't know.
You never came to me,
This is my fault.

You were left to struggle on your own,
You were left in a world of hurt.
To see that hurts me,
To not be able to step in kills me.

My feelings are irrelevant,
This you and I both know.
Your feelings are the most important,
If only you believed though.

My worst day

Through all my struggles it's hard to say
Which for me was truly the worst day.
There have been so many disastrous days,
But one more will end that I can say.
Stress, pain and struggle is all I know,
Down is the only direction I go.
If only things were different, then I'd know,
What was the worst day that I've ever known.

Life is built on experience,
This I know.
There's more to life than existence,
At least I hope.
For now it is darkness,
Just like I've always known.
I bear this weight With sadness,
I carry it alone.

My feelings are in turmoil,
My life in disrepair.
My heart hardly beats,
It's been beaten in there.
My mind is closing in,
It's a war in there.
Overall I'm falling with nobody to care.

I should have listened to my mother

I should have listened to my mother,
She told me to think before I act.
After all the struggles in life, I wish I could take my
thoughtless actions back,
But I can't so that's that.

Running this race of life,
Leaves you feeling like you just might,
Get up and disappear into the night.
I don't want to do that, I know it's not right.
But here I am thinking I just might.

A life of bad decisions,
Thrown in with indecision,
Mixed up with a total lack of precision,
Has left my soul feeling like I'm missing.

It's too late to change the past,
But I need to move fast to make the future last,
And indeed to watch the present pass.
Life could have been easier, it could have been a
blast.

Final payment

One day I may be made to pay.
To pay for the crimes of my past
To pay for all the pieces of a broken heart
To pay for it all.
If I could travel through time and change the past I
would.
I would repair and repay all the damage that I
caused.
I would undo all the destruction
And bring order to the chaos
Unfortunately, I am unable to travel back in time,
Instead, I am just waiting.
Waiting for the day they come and take me
For the day I have to give retribution
For the day I have to forfeit my own life
For the day I get what I'm owed
For the day you get what you need
On that day it will be the end of me.

Running and running

Should I listen to this devil that lives within?
Should I let my anger out?
Or should I hold it in?
All these thoughts and feelings are making my
head ring.
I'd love an easy ride,
to feel free enough to sing.

But instead, I am stuck with this devil battling
within.
It's a war of attrition, one that no matter what
nobody can win.
It's a terrible position that we all find ourselves in.
You run the race wrong when you enter to win.
It's time to change tactics, you can't possibly
sustain and survive the sprint.

The most prolific killer of all

Life is costly, With all the time we take.
We spend our lives worrying about what we'll
make.
But when it's all said and done it's all about the total
spend.
We have a finite amount, And none to lend.
As sad as it is, time kills us all in the end.
So spend it wisely and create no waste.
Enjoy what you have and forgo the haste.

Letter to my children

To me you are my world,
My only reason for existence.
But you seem so unhappy,
Is there something I'm missing?
Do you have what you need?
If not then tell me, I will listen.
Do you need more love?
More than is given?
Do you need a helping hand?
Or are you strong and Indipendant?
Do you need more support?
Or is that already given?
Do you need space?
Or is too much the issue?
When I see you hurting,
I need you to tell me something.
To me you are my world,
Far more than just my children.

Abandonment of self

Who am I?
Am I a person I like?
Or am I the living embodiment of all I despise?

Do I get to choose?
Or do you decide?

Am I judged on my actions?
Or on the person inside?

What if the outcome is negative when we decide?
Do I give up who I am?

Abandon myself for your adoration,
Or continue on as me despite your abhorrence?

Beauty is fleeting

They say beauty is in the eye of the beholder,
And sorrow is in the heart of the sufferer.
But as I grow weary and older,
With the weight of the world on my shoulders,
I often stop to wonder,
Is this life the same for me as it is for the others?
Do they feel the pain that flows through me?
Or do they look on in wonder?
Are you proud to be my friend?
Or will you turn on me in the end?

I just don't know...

When can I rest?
When all the work is done?
Or when all has fallen around me?

Can I stop now?
Or do I have to keep going?
Do I have to keep struggling?
Or am I allowed some peace?

I need to know,
I need my questions answered.
I need your permission for me to stop,
Because it's hard work putting you on top.

Being a man

In life I struggle,
To share my feelings with others.
My logical facade,
Is the flimsiest of covers.
Underneath rages a fire of emotion.
I find myself incapable of release.
I find myself living without peace

When I write my heart does the work.
When the pen hits the paper
My emotions escape with a relentless flow.
I spill it all and out it comes.
Waves of feeling that I cannot control.
Rapid flows of pain and joy crashing into one
another.

If only I could talk to people like I can to paper.
Maybe then I'd be a better man
Instead of a lost little boy with nobody to hold my
hand.

The burden of who I am

All I do is fight,
It is ingrained in my soul.
To stand up for myself,
To defend my position,
To me is all I know.

I am tired now,
I just want to lay down,
To accept oppression in my heart.
To give up being me.

I am trapped,
Leaning on who I am,
While being crushed by how I feel.
I am losing this fight.
I have lost.

My war with indifference

When I am lost,
My identity cannot be found.
When I am down,
The sky cannot be seen.
For right now I am swimming in the sea.
A sea of indifference.
Truly a dangerous place to be.
I could be happy,
I could be sad.
But no,
I am just...

The world as I feel it

It's a dog eat dog world,
Or so they say.
But for me it is worse, unending pain.
I feed the dogs and provide them with support.
But when it comes to reciprocation, those dogs fall
short.

Do I deserve to get the love I give, back?
Or do I deserve the pain of this knife in my back?
Should I be the enemy?
Or am I allowed allies?
Wherever I draw the line I am the only one on my
side.

Nobody to help me,
And nobody to care.
When I fall down I can count on the floor for
support.
When you fall down you have me for support.
I catch you when you are falling, and save you from
impact.

I stand you up and I dust you off.
I wipe away your tears with nothing but love.
You look up at me with disdain before you run off.
It hurts me badly and it cuts me deep.
But never in your life will you care when I weep.

Why do I do it, I hear you ask.

But explaining myself is an easy task.
I treat others how I want to be treated myself.
Even if reciprocation is never felt.

I will never get treatment for my broken heart.
My feelings are deep,
And indeed heavy.
I carry it on my shoulders even though I'm not
ready.

I hold it up for you on a daily basis.
Atlas had the world on his shoulders,
That's an easy job for him.
I carry eternity, and a fight I'll never win.

Printed in Great Britain
by Amazon

26977193R10020